TO: _Mom_

May these words
of inspiration encourage you.

FROM: _Matt & Kimberly_

Moms are a gift from the LORD.

Heartfelt Devotions for Moms

ZondervanPublishingHouse

Grand Rapids, Michigan

A Division of HarperCollinsPublishers

Fruity Folks

The fruit of the Spirit is love, joy, peace, patience, kindness, goodness, faithfulness, gentleness and self-control.

Galatians 5:22–23a

♥

Devotion

The fruit of the Spirit is God's nature exhibited in us. It's what we are when we're like God.

Now, when we start to grow God's characteristics we don't lose our own personalities. The fruit of the Spirit is indeed God's characteristics—but . . . exhibited in our own unique personalities. Whether we're like bananas with sensitive skin protecting an easy-to-bruise interior or the coconut with a hard-as-a-rock exterior covering sweet meat within, when we're alive in the Spirit, God's nature is exhibited through the person he has made us to be.

Prayer

Dear Lord, help me exhibit the fruit of the Spirit by living a more godly life; showing my children your love, joy, peace, patience, kindness, goodness, faithfulness, gentleness, and self-control. Amen.

From Start To Finish

Therefore he is able to save completely those who come to God through him, because he always lives to intercede for them.

Hebrews 7:25

Devotion

When God starts something, he finishes it.... He gives life and ushers it out. He allows us to sin and then he dies on the cross to forgive us for our sins so that we might be restored.

No matter how you fall today, Mom, Jesus saves you *completely*. Even if you lose your temper with your three-year-old or simply dislike your in-laws, or snarl at your husband. Whether you feel his salvation or not, when you trust in him as your Savior and Lord, Jesus saves you *completely*. God finishes what he starts.

Prayer

Dear Lord, I may have failed today in showing love, patience and gentleness, but thank you that I have the assurance of your love and forgiveness because of my trust in Jesus as Savior and Lord. Amen.

Silence!

My soul finds rest in God alone; my salvation comes from him.

Psalm 62:1

❤

Devotion

Ah. Beautiful, quiet silence. When is the last time you heard it?

Sit on the stairs late at night after—finally—getting them all to bed. Listen to the stillness of your home. Turn off the radio in the car after dropping the children off somewhere and take in the quiet. In unexpected moments of aloneness—when you're sitting at a red light and your baby is asleep in his carseat, when you wake early for some reason one morning and no one else is yet stirring—resist the urge to fill the silence with noise. Pray. Listen.

Prayer

Dear God, in the midst of a hectic, noisy day, thank you that my soul can find its rest in you alone. Amen.

What Are You Wearing Today?

Therefore, as God's chosen people, holy
and dearly loved, clothe yourselves with compassion,
kindness, humility, gentleness and patience.

Colossians 3:12

Devotion

Are you clothed in kindness today?

To be kind to another means to be useful to her, to meet a need in her life. You see, kindness is an action. It's the outer expression of inner goodness.... [Paul] suggests that we be clothed with compassion and kindness.

When you get up in the morning, put on your glasses so that you can see. But then go to the closet and find a garment of kindness.... Express goodness in compassionate action by being kind.

Prayer

Dear Lord, I commit to you today to not only open my eyes and recognize the needs around me, but to go a step further and act on those needs, clothed in your love and compassion. Amen.

From Fearful To Faithful

Do not fear, for I am with you; do not be dismayed, for I am your God. I will strengthen you and help you.

Isaiah 41:10

❤

Devotion

What are you afraid of? That your child will reject your faith? That your husband will leave you? That you will lose your job? That you'll remain single for the rest of your life? That you'll die?

Fear is unfaith. It's seeing only what makes human sense in a given situation. The way out of fear is faith.... When you fear, you don't believe. And when you don't believe, you fear.

Prayer

Dear Lord, show me where I need to believe you and what you are saying to me. I want to give up my fear and let you replace it with faith. Amen.

Undying Devotion

Place me like a seal over your heart, like a seal on your arm;
for love is as strong as death, its jealousy unyielding as the grave.

Song of Songs 8:6

Devotion

In the days of mothering, it's tough to keep our attention on marriage. We're busy with the kids. Their needs. Their messes. Their cries. Add a husband to our load, and we feel weighed under.

But the Bible speaks of the potential for marriage when it spells out the nature of marital love. While we may be bent under the strain of children, you and I need the love of our marriages. And so do our husbands.

Prayer

Dear Lord, even when I feel overwhelmed in these busy days of mothering, help me remember that demonstrating love for my husband is essential to the happiness of our family as a whole. Amen.

Teaching My Child About Joy

*A cheerful look brings joy to the heart,
and good news gives health to the bones.*

Proverbs 15:30

❧ ♥ ❧

Devotion

The philosopher, Friedrich Nietzsche, once criticized Christians by saying,
"I would believe in their salvation if they looked a little more like people who
have been saved."

Joy is more than happiness.... Where happiness is circumstantial, joy is
not. Joy is an unshakable confidence in the truths of God, despite circumstances. When our children see an unshakable confidence in the life of one
who says she knows God personally, they are impressed and drawn to know
him themselves.

Prayer

Dear Lord, please give my child a reason to taste the true joy of being confi-
dent in you. Amen.

Love Is A Choice

God is love. Whoever lives in love
lives in God, and God in him.

1 John 4:16b

Devotion

The Bible says that God is love. It also says that we love because God first loved us. If love is a choice for him, it is a choice for us as well. At times it's an easy choice that costs us little and brings much satisfaction. But at other times, choosing to love means choosing to make ourselves open to hurt and rejection.

Prayer

Dear Lord, during those early moments of falling in love with my little ones the choice was easy. Now, when the days become more challenging, help me to still choose love. Amen.

Laughing Matters

Sarah said, "God has brought me laughter, and everyone who hears about this will laugh with me."

Genesis 21:6

❤

Devotion

Sarah learned to laugh at the unexpected turns of her days. At first she laughed rather inappropriately *at* God . . . when she first heard that she would bear a child in her nineties. . . . Later she laughed *with* God out of pure joy at the pain of remembering her doubt of God's power and provision as she held Isaac.

There are so many heavy challenges in life! Will my toddler ever be potty-trained? How will I make it through the years of puberty with a eye-rolling tweenager? . . . The next time you lack perspective on the chaos of your days, consider the lighter side of life: find something to laugh about!

Prayer

"In my heart a melody is ringing with a joy that never will depart; and an angel song could not be sweeter than the song that's ringing in my heart."

—*John W. Peterson (Taken from* Great Hymns of the Faith, *Compiled and edited by John W. Peterson, Copyright 1968 by Singspiration, Inc.)*

A Time to Play

Do you not know that your body is a temple of the Holy Spirit, who is in you, whom you have received from God?

1 Corinthians 6:19

Devotion

Doctors, psychologists, and other experts knowingly tout the benefits of physical fitness on general well-being. Bottom-line, when we're out of shape, we don't feel good and tire easily. In short, we're wretched to live with!

For many of us with overcrowded schedules, physical fitness is one of the first things to go. We figure no one will notice. Wrong. Whether or not the lack of love for our bodies shows on the outside, the inside suffers. And eventually, the damage will be demonstrated in the form of impatience, irritability, and general grouchiness. If a woman doesn't feel good about herself, she's less likely to treat others with goodness.

Prayer

Dear Lord, I want to bear the fruit of goodness, and I recognize that keeping my body physically fit can directly affect my behavior toward others. Amen.

A Legacy Of Hope

And let us consider how we may spur
one another on toward love and good deeds.

Hebrews 10:24

❤

Devotion

How easy it is to leave a trail of pessimism behind us as moms. We're tired.
We get grumpy.

    With careful determination, we can replace the pessimism with hope.
How? Follow the advice of the writer of Hebrews.... Take your children with
you to visit a sick friend. Let them watch you put love in action. Teach
manners to your little ones.... Pray with your children for those you love,
Grandma's and Grandpa's, neighbors, each other.

    It doesn't take much to create a legacy of hope in place of pessimism.
But it does take thought and determination.

Prayer

Dear Lord, show me how I might spur my little ones on toward love in good
deeds by demonstrating how to put love into action. Amen.

Getting The Grade:
Facing The Tests Of Life

Then the LORD said to Satan, "Have you considered my servant Job? There is no one on earth like him; he is blameless and upright."

Job 1:8a

Devotion

Unemployment. Divorce. Secondary infertility. The death of a father. The illness of a child. The cruelty of an acquaintance. There comes a time when our faith is tested deliberately by God—not so we will be overcome—but that we might grasp the validity of our faith and know it to be real. From God's hand comes the cumulative exam designed to layer our learning about him and his work in our lives.

Prayer

Dear Lord, help me to remain faithful. I want to meet your test not with the bleary eyes of a worried novice, but with the confidence of a student who is well-acquainted with the words of her Professor. Amen.

Teaching Our Child To Be Kind

*And God raised us up with Christ... in order that
in the coming ages he might show the incomparable riches
of his grace, expressed in his kindness to us in Christ Jesus.*

Ephesians 2:6–7

Devotion

God wants his people to be good. He's pleased when our goodness illustrates him to those around us. But goodness isn't enough.... In addition to being good, we need to be kind.

Goodness recognizes a need. Kindness meets it.... Goodness realizes there's a job to be done. Kindness does the job.

Prayer

Dear Lord, please teach my child to demonstrate goodness by being kind. As you work in her life to make her good—more like you—please make her nice as well. Amen.

Gentle Mothering?

But we were gentle among you,
like a mother caring for her little children.

1 Thessalonians 2:7

Devotion

When Paul searches for a metaphor to describe his ministry intentions to
the Thessalonians, he selects that of a mother caring for her children—
gently.... *Gently?* Most of us wouldn't pick that adverb to describe our
mothering. Well, maybe when the baby is finally asleep and we tip toe to the
crib and *gently* lower him.... Or when we *gently* comb tangles from our
sensitively-scalped daughter's hair while she twists and whines. And when
we *gently* remind our sixteen-year-old that she'd better be home by curfew.

Maybe Paul *was* onto something here after all. Yep. Gently just about
says it all when it comes to mothering.

Prayer

Dear Lord, it's meaningful that Paul likens his caring to that of mothering.
I want to be the kind of gentle mother that Paul mentions in this passage.
Amen.

There's No Place Like Home

Lord, you have been our dwelling place
throughout all generations.

Psalm 90:1

❤

Devotion

The couch doesn't match the drapes. . . . Out front a collection of Big Wheels and bikes sprawl across a patch of grass. Below the front door lies a cheery mat reading in embellished cursive, "WELCOME." And that's just how we feel inside this well-worn house. . . . Here is peace and safety because here is home and there's no place like home.

Whether in a posh, palatial, well-coordinated home or in a humble bungalow, we can find the home of our dreams when we find it in God. When we find rest in the presence of God, we know for certain that there's no place like home.

Prayer

Dear Lord, thank you that in your presence I can find the safety and peace I long for. You are my refuge, my dwelling place. Amen.

Give A Good Impression Of God

It has given me great joy to find some of your children
walking in the truth, just as the Father commanded us.

2 John 4

❤

Devotion

It is in the home that the first, and perhaps most lasting impression of God is created. What kind of image are your children learning from you?

Do you show your children and your spouse a God who gives unlimited forgiveness by your readiness to let go of resentment?... Do you communicate God's unceasing availability by welcoming the interruptions of young minds and the questions constantly erupting from their days of discovery? What kind of image of God lives within the walls of your home?

Prayer

Dear Lord, help me to give a good impression of God to my children by demonstrating the fruits of the Spirit within the walls of my home. Amen.

Joy, Joy, Joy

This day is sacred to our Lord. Do not grieve,
for the joy of the LORD is your strength.

Nehemiah 8:10b

Devotion

Joy is more than happiness. The word "happiness" comes from the root, "hap," which means "chance." While happiness is circumstantial, joy is not. The Old Testament describes joy as a quality of life as well as an emotion. Joy is a deep confidence in God despite circumstances.

    If we want our neighbors, our relatives, our co-workers, and our children to believe in our God, we'll need more than a pasted-on smile of chance happiness. We'll need *joy:* a confidence in God despite circumstance.

Prayer

Dear Lord, help me try to convince a needy world that true joy does not depend on circumstance but comes from my confidence in you. Amen.

Choosing Love

So if you consider me a partner,
welcome him as you would welcome me.

Philemon 17

Devotion

When you've been wronged, it's pretty tough to muster up feelings of love for the one who's offended you. When your child arrives home for dinner two hours late and you've been on the phone scouring the neighborhood for him, love isn't on your short list of immediate responses.

While defense may be one way to handle hurt, a method which promises more healing is forgiveness.... Remember how much you've needed forgiveness. Review your own errors and those of another may not look so bad.

Paul asked Philemon not just to take runaway slave Onesimus back, but to love him as a part of his own family.

Prayer

Dear Lord, while it may not be the most natural response after an offense, I know that love is the most healing. Amen.

How Good Is God?

*I know that my Redeemer lives, and
that in the end he will stand upon the earth.*

Job 19:25

Devotion

Ask any mom what she is teaching her child and on her list will be something like, "to be good." We have to try to be good. But God doesn't. His being is perfect.

God is good in his actions. When the Bible says that God is good, it implies that God is willing to act on behalf of his people. His actions are always consistent with his purpose to conform his children to his likeness.

Prayer

Dear God, I praise you for your goodness, that you are perfect. Thank you for expressing your good character in good actions which are aimed at my growth and conformity to you. Amen.

What Are You Waiting For?

I waited patiently for the LORD;
he turned to me and heard my cry.

Psalm 40:1

Devotion

We wait for everything. For the dryer to finish. For our husband to get home. For the phone to ring. For the baby to wake. For a car to pull up, returning our child safely home. For a job. For answers to prayer.

With so much experience, we're remarkably unskilled at waiting well.... But the fact is that while we are waiting, God is working. To move us to where he wants us to be. To readjust the lives of others so that his ultimate desires will be fulfilled. To bring about what will make us eventually Christlike, though not necessarily immediately comfortable.

Prayer

Dear Lord, help me to be more skilled at waiting patiently. Thank you that while I am waiting, you are working in my life. Amen.

Faithful Fulfillment

*Now faith is being sure of what we
hope for and certain of what we do not see.*

Hebrews 11:1

Devotion

God is faithful. He fulfills all his promises and completes all his commitments. Are we faithful in return? . . . As he keeps his promises to us, we mirror his faithfulness by keeping ours to him.

We exhibit the fruit of faithfulness by being obedient to what we read in his Word. . . . We are faithful to God when we are dependable to others. There in the morning when your child awakens. Willing to make a batch of cookies at an unreal hour with no warning. Continuing in prayer when a rebellious heart ignores the voice of our God.

Prayer

Dear God, thank you that you are faithful. You fulfill all your promises and complete all your commitments. Help me to be faithful in return. Amen.

Lighting The World

The LORD is my light and my salvation—whom shall I fear?

Psalm 27:1

Devotion

How has the Lord been your light? Has he given you courage to talk about the tough things? Has he comforted you in loss?

You can find simple ways to shine God's love into the darkness of those around you. Sharing a meal with a family when a new baby arrives. Swapping kids and babysitting for each other. Telling of a book you found helpful, teaching how to wallpaper, cut children's hair, arrange a room to save space.

People need the Lord. Will you be his light in their darkness?

Prayer

Dear Lord, help me be a light to those living in darkness in our world—those I meet in my neighborhood, in the grocery store, in the park. Amen.

Teaching My Child About Love

This is how we know what love is: Jesus Christ laid down his life for us. And we ought to lay down our lives for our brothers.

1 John 3:16

Devotion

Love may make the world go 'round, but not without a lot of work. In 1 John 3:16–17 it is clear that love must be put in action. Only by practicing love can we move towards understanding it fully.

Love is a skill that requires a lot of work. By practicing it and purifying it, we can aim towards perfecting it.

Prayer

Dear Lord, please help my child learn to love others with the love you have shown her. Give her opportunities to perfect the skill of love. Amen.

To Settle or To Win?

[Love] is not rude, it is not self-seeking,
it is not easily angered, it keeps no record of wrongs.

1 Corinthians 13:5

Devotion

When you're working out a struggle with a child, with a spouse, with a neighbor, or with a coworker, one practical principle will take you a long way towards peace: when you're fighting, get your goal straight. Do you want to settle the argument or do you want to win?

The language of love is spelled out in the word compromise.... Ogden Nash provides a modern-day translation of this text saying, "When you're wrong, admit it. When you're right, shut up!"

Prayer

The next time I find myself slugging it out to win, help me to submit my need for victory to the greater value of love—to settle, not to win. Amen.

Fruit That Lasts

You did not choose me, but I chose you and
appointed you to go and bear fruit—fruit that will last.

John 15:16

Devotion

We look about our lives for some measurement that we're making a differ-
ence. We need not look far. In her address to the 1990 graduating class of
Wellesley College, this line drew then-First Lady Barbara Bush the most
fervent applause: "At the end of your life, you'll never regret not having passed
one more test, not winning one more verdict, or not closing one more deal.
You will regret times not spent with a husband, a friend, a child, or a parent."

Prayer

Dear Lord, when I feel torn between the many responsibilities in my day,
help me remember that the only "fruit" in this lifetime that will last to the
next is the "fruit" of relationship. Amen.

A Search for Joy

You will fill me with joy in your presence,
with eternal pleasures at your right hand.

Psalm 16:11b

Devotion

Where do we find joy? In days where the only music in our ears is the ten minutes of silence when our toddler naps in his carseat between errands, where do we find joy? We find it where the quote tells us: in God's presence.

If you want joy, read your Bible, not just a devotional. Read the actual words of God in the pages of the Bible. Take a few small bits of Scripture with your morning coffee, while you shower, as you drive in the car or before you turn out the lights at night.

Prayer

"Thy Word is like a garden, Lord, with flowers bright and fair; and ev'ryone who seeks may pluck a lovely cluster there. Thy Word is like a deep, deep mine, and jewels rich and rare are hidden in its mighty depths for ev'ry searcher there."

—*Edwin Hodder*

A Picture Of Peace

[Jesus] got up, rebuked the wind and said
to the waves, "Quiet! Be still!" Then the wind
died down and it was completely calm.

Mark 4:39

Devotion

The story is told of a king who held a contest to find the perfect painting of peace.... The winning painting depicted a raging storm on a mountainside. Lodged in a crevice, a mother bird sat on her nest, protecting her young. Such a picture of peace resembles the one we're given in Mark 4:35–41.

    Peace is Jesus asleep in a boat in the middle of a storm. Peace is a calm trust in God in the midst of, rather than in the absence of, irritation.

Prayer

Dear Lord, thank you for the peace you offer through your control over every detail of life; for peace even when the world about us screams that there is no reason to believe. Amen.

Gentlewomen

*But the fruit of the Spirit is . . . gentleness and
self-control. Against such things there is no law.*

Galatians 5:22–23

Devotion

The Bible makes much of gentleness. But the biblical brand of gentleness is a
tough term to define.

When we look at the historical background of this word gentleness, we
get a picture that is not weak but is rather, harnessed power. It is a bent will.
Taken from the picture of the wild animal tamed to reach its potential,
gentleness is a soul that has been harnessed and bent to serve the will of God.

Prayer

Dear Lord, that's the kind of gentlewoman I'd like to be. Please give me
gentleness and self-control to serve the will of God in my responsibilities as
a mother. Amen.

Mature Trees

They will still bear fruit in old age,
they will stay fresh and green.

Psalm 92:14

Devotion

Laps open and ready for watching post-nap cartoons. . . . Checks hidden in birthday cards. Games played on tables still sticky from holiday baking. Wrinkly hands curled atop piano keys while others gather 'round to listen.

Grandmothers. Some advanced in years. Others still mother-like themselves. All, bringing an offering that can be duplicated by no other. An offering of wisdom that comes from living life long, of patience that has grown out of trial and of laughter that has been learned through integrating the fat with the lean times.

Prayer

Dear Lord, I pray that I may someday have the privilege of showing my grandchildren your love as I continue bearing fruit in old age. Amen.

Love Means Saying, "I'm Sorry"

Create in me a pure heart, O God,
and renew a steadfast spirit within me.

Psalm 51:10

Devotion

The words escaped from your lips and sliced, like a sword, at your husband's heart. Your temper flared and your voice rose, and now your two-year-old is hunkered down at your feet, crying.

Love means taking the responsibility for your errors and admitting them, first to yourself, then to God, and then taking the final step by admitting them to the one you've wronged. No, an apology may not magically make it all better. But it is a beginning.

Prayer

Dear Lord, it's not easy to apologize, but please give me the courage to admit my errors and show my love by offering an apology to those I've wronged. Amen.

The Towel Brigade

I have set you an example that
you should do as I have done for you.

John 13:15

❤

Devotion

Not long before his death, Jesus gathered his disciples together for some last minute instructions. To begin the lesson, he used a teaching aid. To illustrate the extent to which the Son of God would serve man, Jesus wrapped a towel about his waist, bent down, and cleaned the filthy feet of his friends.

Are you a member of the "towel brigade"? Do your children see you stoop to wash—with an attitude of love? Is your husband a recipient of your servant touch? Take up your towel and wash!

Prayer

Dear Lord, thank you for your example of how to love others. Help me demonstrate your love to others in the practicality of everyday life. Amen.

Keep It In Perspective

*Better a dry crust with peace and quiet than
a house full of feasting with strife.*

Proverbs 17:1

Devotion

It is so easy to trundle down the path of the insignificant! ... Throwing a
tantrum over a husband's tardiness, thus setting the rest of the evening on
edge. Battling over a bath when a sticky, happy child would rather go to
bed dirty.

In some moments, these issues might matter. But in the long run, how
much? The next time you catch yourself spinning out in a frenzy ask one
simple question, "Will this matter in five years?" If so, focus your energy on
completing what is before you with grace and efficiency. If not, forget it.

Prayer

Dear Lord, help me to focus on the eternal rather than the insignificant
when I begin to feel overwhelmed. Amen.

Teaching My Child
About God's Goodness

You are good, and what you do is good; teach me your decrees.

Psalm 119:68

Devotion

When the Bible says that God is good, what does it mean? First, God is good in his being. Second, God is good in his actions.... His actions are always consistent with his purpose of conforming his children to his likeness.

Sometimes we enjoy God's goodness. At other times, we question it. For just as he is good to give us what makes us happy, he is happy to give us what will make us good.

Prayer

Dear Lord, please show your goodness to my child. When my child struggles along in situations that are tough to endure, show him that you are good then too. Amen.

Perfect Peace

*You will keep in perfect peace him whose
mind is steadfast, because he trusts in you.*

Isaiah 26:3

Devotion

The camera spans a spacious, private bath scene, circulating around a tub filled to the brim with luxurious bubbles. It rests upon beautiful woman, hair pinned in loose curls, arms extended, massaging shapely legs, eyes closed in an ecstasy of relaxation.

Contrary to the commercial, peace doesn't come in a package of bubble bath. Peace comes when we fix our minds on God and on his stability in our chaotic days. No matter what mess is tromping across our floors or standing at our doors, the unchangeable God is in charge of our days. Knowing that for a fact is peace.

Prayer

"Like a river glorious is God's perfect peace, over all victorious in its bright increase; perfect, yet it floweth fuller ev'ry day, perfect, yet it groweth deeper all the way."

—*Frances R. Havergal*

The King's Kindness

But when the kindness and love of God our
Savior appeared, he saved us, not because of righteous
things we had done, but because of his mercy.

Titus 3:4–5a

Devotion

In the morning we determine to keep our voices at a reasonable decibel the entire day but by nine-thirty, we're already hollering at the kids.... We desperately want to be kind but we don't know how.

If you want to be kind to others then begin by accepting the King's kindness for yourself. Until we've experienced it firsthand, it's pretty tough to extend it to others. It's the kindness of God which draws us out of our tainted world back into a relationship with him.

Prayer

Oh God, thank you for expressing your kindness in the gift of your Son, Jesus, dying for our sins so that we might be restored in a relationship with you. Amen

Life's Vital Ingredient

I will sing of the LORD's great love forever; with my mouth
I will make your faithfulness known through all generations.

Psalm 89:1

Devotion

Without love, humans will die. It's that simple.

Decades ago an experiment was performed that today underlines the most vital ingredients in healthful human development. In an orphanage, half the infants were cuddled and snuggled by the caretakers, while the other half received only the most rudimentary attention through feedings and changings. Within a few short weeks the unattended, unloved, untouched babies began to show signs of failure to thrive. Without love, their lives waned.

Prayer

Thank you, dear God, for your unconditional love, filling to the brim my insatiable desire for personal acceptance. Amen.

Your Family's Coat Of Arms

"Stand at the crossroads and look; ask for the ancient paths, ask where the good way is, and walk in it, and you will find rest for your souls."

Jeremiah 6:16

Devotion

If you had a coat of arms for your family today, what would it communicate about your family? Is yours a tapestry woven with the fruits of love, joy, peace, patience and kindness? Do the threads of your spiritual heritage, as passed down from generation to generation, show through? Do the symbols demonstrate a faith that expresses itself in action in the lives of those around you?

Prayer

"O give us homes with godly fathers, mothers, who always place their hope and trust in Him; whose tender patience turmoil never bothers, whose calm and courage trouble cannot dim; a home where each finds joy in serving others, and love still shines, tho days be dark and grim."

—*Barbara B. Hart*

Have You Ever Been Hungry?

*For I was hungry and you gave me something
to eat, I was thirsty and you gave me something to
drink, I was a stranger and you invited me in.*

Matthew 25:35

Devotion

Has there been a time in your life when you didn't have enough to eat?
When the only coat you possessed was two sizes too small? Perhaps you are
in a position to say no to these questions. But a growing number of adults
and children are experiencing hunger and physical need as never before.

As we give to others, we give to Jesus. Take your children's hands. Lead
them to their closets and their toy boxes. Teach them now to share with
others from what they have.

Prayer

Dear Lord, I want to teach my children to love Jesus by loving their world.
Make me aware of those who are in need of our help. Amen.

Teaching My Child Self-Control

*Better a patient man than a warrior, a man
who controls his temper than one who takes a city.*

Proverbs 16:32

Devotion

Peter the Great was the maker of Czarist Russia. He captured city upon city, but he never was able to hold his temper. Once, in a fit of rage, he murdered his own son. Near the end of his reign he commented, "I have conquered an empire, but I was not able to conquer myself."

Most literally, the word *self-control* comes from two roots: one meaning to "rein in" or "curb" and the other meaning to "heal," "preserve," "make whole." . . . Putting it more simply, to be self-controlled is to be healthy-minded.

Prayer

Dear Lord, may I be a model of self-control that my child might see in me an accurate reflection of this quality and how to put it into practice in everyday life. Amen.

Special Service

For even the Son of Man did not come to be served,
but to serve, and to give his life as a ransom for many.

Mark 10:45

Devotion

"What can I do to help?" We ask the question all the time. The answer is simple. Keep your service special.

For someone who is sick: take a meal in a disposable container, calling ahead to check out likes and dislikes and a convenient delivery time.... For someone who is grieving: make a personal visit. Sit and listen.... For the poor: contribute money through your church or to a parachurch ministry which works directly with the poor. Volunteer to help in an inner city health clinic. Tutor adults in reading programs.

Prayer

Dear Lord, help me to be more effective in my service by finding ways to make it special. Amen.